The River That Wolves Moved

A True Tale from Yellowstone

Written by Mary Kay Carson and Illustrated by David Hohn

"Look deep into nature, and then you will understand everything better."

—Albert Einstein

This is the **river** that wolves moved.

This is the **pack**, so furry and fast,
That hunts near the river that wolves moved.

Yellowstone was without wolves for more than 70 years. Then, in 1995, wolves were set free in the national park. These gray wolves quickly grouped into packs, started hunting, and had pups. Eight or so wolf packs patrol the park today. Each pack has 11 to 12 wolves.

These are the **elk**, watchful and strong,
Who are prey for the pack
That hunts near the river that wolves moved.

When wolves were gone, elk had fewer predators to worry about. Large herds gathered in river valleys near fresh water, tasty plants, and tender trees. Once wolves were back on the prowl, elk became prime prey. The hunted herds grew smaller. Now the elk watch out for wolves and keep on the move.

These are the **willows**, thick-rooted and bushy,
That are chomped on by elk
Who are prey for the pack
That hunts near the river that wolves moved.

Elk used to munch down bush-like thickets of water-loving willow trees. But once the wolves started hunting, there were fewer hungry elk near the river. Willows and other plants and trees grew back. Colorful songbirds now build nests in these trees. The birds search along the river for tasty bugs.

With willows to eat, beavers moved back in and built dams. Beaver dams slow water flow and create pools along rivers. These ponds become homes for frogs, ducks, dragonflies, and other bugs.

This is the **bank**, made of dark muddy soil,
Held in place by the willows
That are chomped on by elk
Who are prey for the pack
That hunts near the river that wolves moved.

A bank is where river meets land, where water touches dirt.
Plant and tree roots grasp the soil, holding riverbanks in place.
When the wolves were gone, the elk feasted on trees, leaving
the riverbanks bare and brown. Rushing water ate at the
banks, creating swift rivers with sharp zigzag turns.

Now that willows and other trees have regrown, riverbanks are stronger. The web of roots helps support and protect the banks from the pushy water. Yellowstone's rivers now flow more slowly in gentler S-shaped curves.

This is the **water** that runs clear and cold,

Flowing in between banks

Held in place by the willows

That are chomped on by elk

Who are prey for the pack

That hunts near the river that wolves moved.

Fast-flowing water carries away bits of rock and soil from the riverbank. This is called erosion and it muddies the water. A riverbank supported by tree and plant roots has less erosion. The grasping roots hold onto soil and help keep the water clear.

These are the **fish**, spotted and sleek,
That glide through the water
Flowing cold between banks
Held in place by the willows
That are chomped on by elk
Who are prey for the pack
That hunts near the river that wolves moved.

Some fish, such as cutthroat trout, only breed in clear, cool water. They lay their eggs on sparkling gravel, not mud-covered riverbeds. Trees also shade the river, keeping its water cool.

This is the **child** in the quiet of dusk
Who seeks the sleek fish
That glide through the water
Flowing cold between banks
Held in place by the willows
That are chomped on by elk
Who are prey for the pack
That hunts near the river that wolves moved.

These are the **wolves** howling a a h h R R O O o o,

That are heard by the child

Who seeks the sleek fish

That glide through the water

Flowing cold between banks

Held in place by the willows

That are chomped on by elk

Who are prey for the pack

That hunts near the river that wolves moved.

Yellowstone's valleys and rivers changed with fewer hungry elk around. Forests of trees and bushes grew back on hillsides and riverbanks. Riverbanks supported by roots eased erosion, clearing the water and slowing its flow. Changes brought on by wolves helped reshape the landscape.

This is the river that wolves moved.

WITHOUT wolves, too many
elk were eating up the plants
that held riverbanks in place.

What causes a river to take a particular path? How steep the land is, rock types, and depth of water all affect where and how a river flows. So do plants, trees, animals, and other living things. An *ecosystem* includes both living and nonliving things interacting in an environment.

Move Rivers?

WITH wolves preying on elk, the riverside plants regrew, changing the path and pace of flowing water. This is how wolves move rivers.

Wolves boost the variety of living things, the *biodiversity*, by preying on elk and coyotes. Fewer elk causes an increase in the kinds of birds, fish, frogs, and plants living along rivers. A smaller number of coyotes means more rabbits and squirrels for foxes, badgers, and golden eagles to hunt.

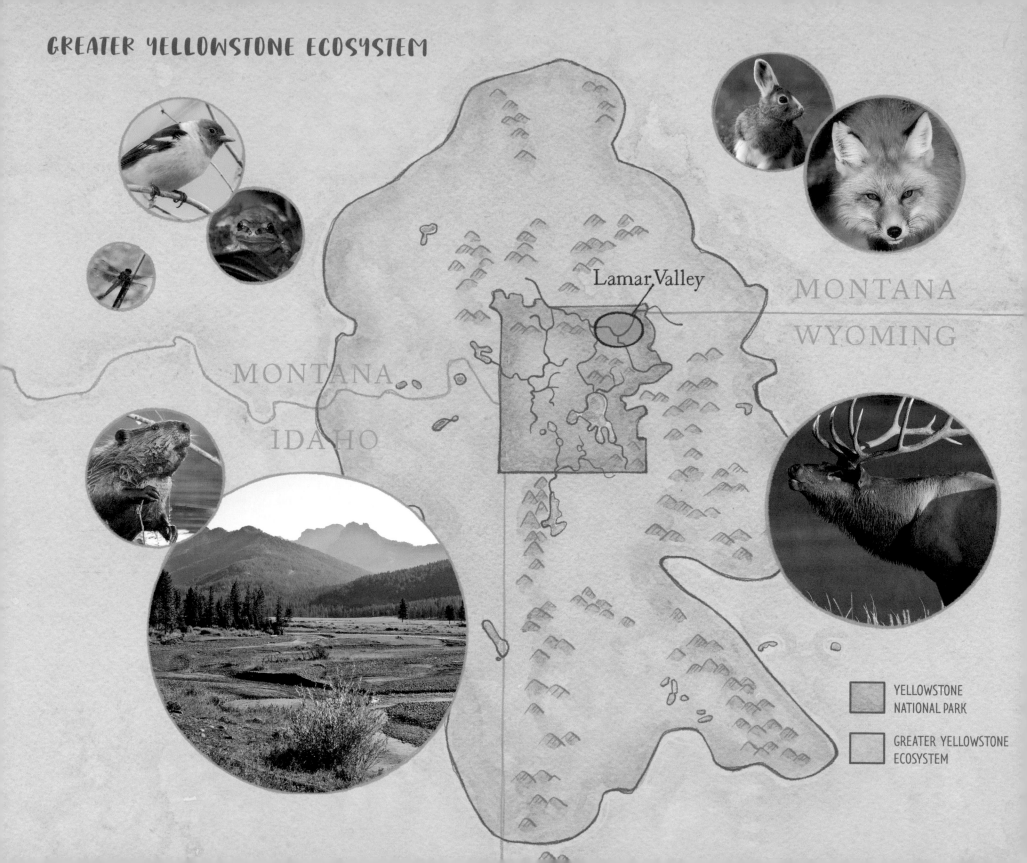

GREATER YELLOWSTONE ECOSYSTEM

Lamar Valley

MONTANA

WYOMING

MONTANA

IDAHO

YELLOWSTONE
NATIONAL PARK

GREATER YELLOWSTONE
ECOSYSTEM

The Wolves of Yellowstone

When Yellowstone National Park was created in 1872, rangers and ranchers legally hunted, trapped, and poisoned wolves. By the early 1900s, all of Yellowstone's wolves were gone. Over time, park scientists learned the importance of predators and decided to bring wolves back. In the winter of 1995, wildlife experts moved 41 wild Canadian wolves into the park. About 500 gray wolves live in the Greater Yellowstone Ecosystem today. As this book went to print, Yellowstone's wolves face a new threat. Montana and other states bordering the park lifted many hunting restrictions on wolves. Trophy hunters killed more than 20 Yellowstone wolves that wandered outside park boundaries in 2022.

Which River Was Moved by Wolves?

The river illustrated in this book represents any one of a number of Lamar River tributaries in the northeastern corner of Yellowstone National Park's Lamar Valley region where scientists have documented changes in tree and plant growth since wolves were reintroduced.

"Country without wolves isn't really good country. It's incomplete. It doesn't have its full spirit."

—Doug Smith, National Park Service biologist who worked to reintroduce wolves to Yellowstone National Park

To Zelda, a lover of all creatures
—MKC

To Colin, Peter, and Chris. Remembering our childhood trip to Yellowstone.
—DH

SELECTED BIBLIOGRAPHY

Encyclopædia Britannica® Online, s.v. "trophic cascade," by Carpenter, Stephen.
https://www.britannica.com/science/trophic-cascade

Farquhar, Brodie. "Wolf Reintroduction Changes Ecosystem in Yellowstone." Yellowstone National Parks Trips. *Outside* magazine. June 30, 2021
http://www.yellowstonepark.com/wolf-reintroduction-changes-ecosystem/

Monbiot, G. (2013, July). *George Monbiot: For More Wonder, Rewild The World*. TED Conferences, LLC.http://www.ted.com/talks/george_monbiot_for_more_wonder_rewild_the_world

Ranger Q & A: Wolves, Doug Smith. National Park Service. U.S. Department of the Interior.
https://www.nps.gov/yell/learn/photosmultimedia/qa-wolves.htm

Ripple, W.J., Beschta, R.L. Trophic cascades in Yellowstone: The first 15 years after wolf reintroduction.
Biol. Conserv. (2011), doi:10.1016/j.biocon.2011.11.005

Wolves in Yellowstone. National Park Service. U.S. Department of the Interior.
https://www.nps.gov/yell/learn/nature/wolves.htm